CW00924543

WALKING
❖ IN ❖
DIVINE
FAVOR

JERRY SAVELLE

WALKING IN DIVINE FAVOR

ISBN 0-9655352-0-7
Unless otherwise stated, all Scripture
quotations are taken from
The King James Version of the Bible.

Jerry Savelle Publications

From   **JSMI(UK)**
School Hill Centre
Chepstow, Monmouthshire
NP16 5PH
UK
Tel: +44(0)1291 628074

C   le

TABLE OF CONTENTS

1

❧

You're Somebody Special To God

You've Been Crowned With Glory & Honor

Have you ever felt like a failure in life? Have you ever experienced insecurity? Insecurity about your appearance, your abilities, your personality, your life? Have you ever felt unloved and worthless? *I'm not attractive. I can't do all the things that person can do. I'm not good enough! Nothing good ever happens in my life. I'm a failure.*

If your mind is filled with thoughts of worthlessness, shame, embarrassment and low self-esteem, then it's time to get rid of that insecurity! "How can I get rid of insecurity that's been there my whole life?" By realizing that YOU are God's most prized-possession! If God had to choose the finest thing He ever created - He'd say YOU! Yes, you! You are somebody special to God.

Those thoughts and feelings are lies from the Devil aimed at getting you so down on yourself that you will never experience God's best for your life. They try to make you feel you are "just not good enough" so why would God want to bless you? God does not have one child who is not good enough to receive His love.

There are a lot of people who never enjoy victories in their lives because of such low self-esteem. Jesus said that we are to love one another even as we love ourselves. If you don't like YOU, how are you ever going to like somebody else?

Low self-esteem is a result of a lack of knowledge. The reason so many Christians live way below their privileges as a child of God is because they don't know that they are highly favored of God.

In Psalm 8:3-5, the psalmist is reflecting on the greatness of God and writes,

> *When I consider thy heavens, the work of thy fingers, the moon and the stars which thou hast ordained; What is man, that thou art mindful of him? and the son of man, that thou visitest him? For thou hast made him a little lower than the angels, and hast crowned him with glory and honour.*

In this particular scripture, the psalmist is overwhelmed at just how marvelous and magnificent God is and with His ability to create the universe. Have you ever just stopped and looked around at God's creation? Just go look at the Grand Canyon some time. It's overwhelming. We get so accustomed to the things around us, but if you take the time to just look at the sky or the sunset and think that God created that - it's amazing!

The Psalmist is saying, "Lord, You're so magnificent and creative, why would You have anything to do with man? Why did You create man?" But God is saying that you are His most prized-possession! In fact, in the mind of God, you are more valuable than the stars, the moon, the heavens, and all His handiwork.

Just like an artist with all the wonderful, creative pieces he designs, there's always this prized-possession. That's the way God feels about YOU! Now, religion doesn't teach us that. Religion wants us to stay in a sinful state. Religion dwells on, *All have sinned and come short of the glory of God.* Well, that's true, but that's also the reason why

Jesus came, because all sinned and fell short of the glory of God. But God didn't leave us that way! He sent Jesus to redeem us from Adam's transgression, and from the curse of the law, and because the blood of Jesus worked, we're not "old sinners" anymore.

Nothing you did in your past could be so terrible that God wouldn't forgive you. You are washed by the blood of Jesus, and made a new creation in Christ Jesus. You have the nature of Almighty God!

You are of a royal family. In the natural, you may have some folks in your family that you're not too proud of, but I'm talking about in the spirit realm. Your ancestry goes all the way back to God. The blood of Jesus flows through your veins. You've got a crown on your head that can't be seen with the natural eye, but it's there. It's a crown of honor, and you need to walk in it.

You are somebody special to God! Don't call yourself a worm in the sight of God. "We're just worms in His sight." No, we're not. You better not be a worm, the Devil will come by and eat thee!

You can't be anything less than a new creation in the sight of God. If you are, then that would mean that the blood of Jesus didn't work, and I wouldn't dare say the blood of Jesus didn't work. It worked. Praise God!

Very importantly, you've got to keep all of this balanced. You can't become high-minded and have the attitude that you're somebody special because of what you did or because of who you are. That has nothing to do with it. Without Jesus, you're nothing! You have no merits, you didn't earn this favor, you didn't earn this honor, Jesus earned it for you. But because of what He did, you can hold your head up high and know that you are deeply loved by God.

When you begin to see yourself the way God sees you (crowned with glory and honor), then you'll begin to expect favor and success. You'll expect every adversity to be turned into victory. You'll expect to have authority over your circumstances, Why? Because you're God's prized-possession.

PREFERENTIAL TREATMENT

There are so many people who don't expect good things to happen to them. In fact, people really get mad at me because they think that I'm too positive. I'm not just a positive thinker; in fact, I'm not dealing with the power of positive thinking. I'm dealing with the power of revelation knowledge. However, when you have something revealed to you from the Word of God, it causes you to become very positive. You'll have a positive attitude, and you'll expect to win in every adversity.

Doubt and insecurity will vanish as you become more and more conscious of just how much favor and honor you have been given by God. John 12:26 says, *...if any man serve me, him will my Father honour.*

If you've chosen to serve Jesus, then Jesus Himself said because of your decision, "My Father will honor you." Hallelujah! When you're honored by someone, then you can expect to receive preferential treatment.

You must begin to walk in your God-given authority. You have authority over the circumstances that seem to be controlling your life; therefore, you should expect, through the Name of Jesus and the Word of God, to change those circumstances into something that turns out for your good.

When you truly know that God has crowned you with glory and honor, then you will walk in an expectancy of good things happening in your life, and no one will be able to convince you otherwise.

THE OBJECT OF GOD'S AFFECTION

Do you feel loved? It's a wonderful thing knowing you're loved. Knowing that there is somebody out there who loves you, who makes you feel good inside. But if you feel unloved and feel that there is absolutely no one who even cares about you, then the lies of the Devil are working in you and creating a deep feeling of loneliness. But listen to this. Even greater than a human being expressing love to you, God says in Numbers 6:25-26 that He will ...*make his face shine upon thee, and be gracious unto thee;* And He will ...*lift up his countenance upon thee, and give thee peace.*

What is He saying? You are the object of His affection. If you were the only human being alive on the planet, God would have sent Jesus to die for you. That's how much you're loved by the Father. I believe many of you reading this book are going to experi-ence a real deliverance simply because you've realized that you are loved and highly favored of God. Even in the hard places, you have this confidence that everything is going to be all right because God is on your side, and He will never let you down.

Do you ever feel alone? Like everyone's against you? Let's find out what happens to people who are loved by God.

> *What shall we then say to these things? If God be for us, who can be against us? He that spared not his own Son, but delivered him up for us all, how shall he not with him also freely give us all things?*
>
> Romans 8:31,32

There are still a lot of Christians who are not convinced that God's for them. They think God's the enemy. How would you like to be commander-in-chief of an army where half of your troops don't even know who the enemy is? They've got their weapons pointed toward headquarters, blaming you all the time for their problems.

There are people always questioning God, "Why did You let this happen to me?" They don't yet realize that God is for them and not against them! God did not cause this awful situation in your life to prove something to you. He cares about you. You are so loved by God that He is willing to give you freely ALL things. He's on your side!

Verse 34 says, *Who is he that condemneth? It is Christ that died...* You shouldn't be walking in condemnation. You shouldn't be listening to the lies of the Devil condemning you all the time and telling you how lousy you are, what a failure and a nobody you are. A person who listens to that all the time does not have a revelation of favor and honor.

You're so highly favored of God that He's saying that no weapon formed against you shall prosper (Isaiah 54:17). You've been justified in the sight of God. NOTHING can separate you from God's love!

> *For I am persuaded, that neither death, nor life, nor angels, nor principalities, nor powers, nor things present, nor things to come, nor height, nor depth, nor any other creature, shall be able to separate us from the love of God, which is in Christ Jesus our Lord.*
>
> Romans 8:38,39

When you become "persuaded" of just how loved you are, and just how valuable you are in the sight of God, then you can say what Paul said, "There is nothing that can separate me from the love of Christ. Not things present nor things to come." Amen!

You are somebody special. Quit running yourself down. Quit talking ugly about yourself. Quit talking about what a failure you are. Don't run yourself down all the time. Don't talk about how unworthy you are. You are the handiwork of God. You are loved. You are highly favored of God.

Expect greater victories in your life because you are favored of God. Don't get discouraged when a storm comes, because you know you're favored of God and some-how, some way God will turn it around! You are crowned with glory and honor. It doesn't matter what your past is like or how many mistakes you've made, you are special to God.

Begin to expect to win in every situation simply because you are highly favored of God. Your life will become enjoyable because you know that God is going to work everything out no matter how impossible it may look. Remember, He's on your side; therefore, you cannot be defeated!

2
❧ ❧

⚜

FAVOR:
A Gift From God

Now that we've dealt with your self-esteem and you now realize how special you are to God, let's define favor. Exactly what is *favor*? *Favor* is *something granted out of good will rather than for justice or payment.* In other words, it is a gift from God. You didn't earn it. You can't buy it. You can't be so good that finally God will say, "You've been so good, you've earned favor." It is also defined as *a gift bestowed as a token of regard, love or friendliness (or friendship) and preferential treatment.* It's what Jesus did at Calvary that earned you the favor of God.

We use this word "favor" in our every day language. Sometimes you ask someone, "Would you do a favor for me?" What are you saying? "Just how strong is our relationship? Is our relationship so strong that you would do this for me without question?" That's a favor. Then we start reading about favor from the Bible and get into a church that has some stained glass windows and some pews, and we think favor has a "religious" meaning, but it's the same thing. In fact, God wants you to ask Him for favors.

Not too long ago, a friend of mine who is a Christian businessman, came to me after a service I was ministering in and said, "Brother Jerry, I really need for you to pray over my business. This thing is falling apart. If God doesn't give us supernatural intervention, we're going to lose it all." He said, "I know God gave me this business and God has blessed me through this business. It is just an all out attack of the Devil."

I've known this man a long time and when he said that, I could sense how overwhelmed he was by this. The compassion of the Lord Jesus began to rise up in me and I took his hand and started praying for him but I heard something come out of me that I don't think I had ever prayed before. I said, "Lord Jesus, as a favor to me, intervene on my friend's behalf."

I don't ever remember a time where I had prayed like that. Usually I'd say, "Father, in the Name of Jesus..." and I'd quote the Word, but I didn't that time. That man called me three days later and said, "God gave us a supernatural breakthrough!" He said, "I don't know what you said, but God came through, hallelujah!"

So, I asked the Lord, "Why did you do that so fast?"

He said, "Because you asked Me for a favor."

I said, "Glory to God, do I carry that much weight with You?"

He said, "You do." He said, "You don't realize it but you have that kind of favor." Then He said, "Wouldn't you do the same thing for Me if I came to you and said, 'Jerry, I need a favor'?" Of course I would!

Religion wants it to be so hard to get the ear of God. Religion wants you to think you've got to be so good, and have all this merit, but the Bible says, "He's full of compassion." I believe many sinners stay sinners because they've had the wrong image of God portrayed to them. Most sinners don't know the goodness of God. All they know about God is what they've heard from most Christians. "Thou shalt not... If thou do, thou shalt die..."

They hear that God is just looking for an opportunity to knock their brains out. That's what I thought before I began serving the

Lord. That's the image that Christians gave me. I thought, "Dear God, I know the Devil is trying to kill me, and now I'm going to serve God and He's going to try to kill me too. I haven't got a chance."

But then I got into the Word of God and found out that I'd been lied to. I found out that God is gracious. God is full of compassion. God is merciful. He's plenteous in mercy and not only that, the nature of God is to show favor.

I found out that the more of the nature of God that is imparted into me as a result of the Word and as a result of fellowship with Him, the more I am disposed to show favors to others. You become like God. You become full of mercy. You become compassionate. You become one from which people can ask favors.

The Lord is merciful and gracious, slow to anger, and plenteous in mercy.

Psalm 103:8

Did you hear that? You're not making God mad all the time. Even when you foul up, God's not saying, "Where's Michael - my war angel... Kill them." No. He's slow to anger. He's a good God.

In the Hebrew, many times the words *mercy* and *compassion* are interchangeable, and, in some cases, defined as *disposed to show favors.* In other words, the very nature of God is disposed to show favor. God can't help Himself. He is so good, He's disposed to show favor.

Psalm 5:12 says,

> *For thou, Lord, wilt bless the right-eous; with favor wilt thou compass him as with a shield.*

The Amplified Bible says,

> *...as with a shield You will sur-round him with good will (pleasure and favor).*

FAVOR: A GIFT FROM GOD

"Pleasure" is an area that religion doesn't teach us either. God does not mind you having pleasure. Religion doesn't want you to have any fun! I'm glad I never became *religious*. I love God with all my heart. I'm sold out and deeply committed to God but I'm not religious. Even before I became a Christian, I've always had somewhat of a joyful nature. I was always the class clown. I was always making folks laugh. It wasn't something I tried to do. It was just my nature.

But when I got around people who tried to get me to become a Christian, I thought, *Dear God, if I ever become a Christian, I'll never laugh again.* Humor seemed to have no place in religion. I thought, *I'll have to change my whole personality if I get saved. I'll have to take on this wrinkled, prune face look...never laugh...never have any joy...just sit in the corner reading the Bible all day - join a convent or become a monk.*

Then I found out that God has a sense of humor. He wanted to change me from death unto life, and He also wanted to use my personality. And He wants to use your personality too! God gave you your personality. So notice, He says, *as with a shield You will surround him with good will (pleasure and favor)* - Psalm 5:12. God will surround you with pleasure. Your Christianity ought to be fun. It ought to be so much fun that sinners become envious.

Now don't think, "Brother Jerry just never has any problems." I have problems just like you. I have adversity just like you. I have opposition just like you. I have to stand on the Word of God constantly, just like you. But the beautiful part is, I know that I have the favor of God and somehow, some way before this thing is all said and done, and before the dust settles, I'll win. I have the favor of God, hallelujah. He's never failed me. Never!

Do you realize what the favor of God will do in your life? It will open doors that men say are impossible to open. It will change rules, regulations, policies and even bring down governments, if necessary, to get you through a door God wants you through. The favor of God will turn every adversity in your life into a victory, praise God.

> *Grace* [or favor] *be with all them that love our Lord Jesus Christ in sincerity.*
>
> Ephesians 6:24

Another word for **grace** is *unmerited favor*. So, when you see the word "grace" you could interchange it with the word "favor." The Apostle Paul says, "For everyone who walks with God and is sincere about that walk, favor be unto them."

Don't get mad at others if doors open for them that don't open to you. You can have preferential treatment too. Don't get mad when others are blessed. You can be just as blessed. Don't get mad because you hear testimonies of wonderful things happening in others' lives. You are highly favored of the Lord, but you need to learn how to walk in divine favor.

The Bible says that God is no respecter of persons. That means that the same preferential treatment they get, you can have too. Obviously, if you don't have a revelation of it, then you can't walk in it. A lack of knowledge will cause you to live way below your privileges. But once you have a revelation of how special you are to God, then you will be able to walk in favor.

Instead of having low self-esteem, no confidence and just taking everything the Devil dishes out, we ought to be walking around with our heads held high knowing full well that we have preferential treatment with Almighty God! You and I are honored by God.

Proverbs 14:9 says,

> *Fools make a mock at sin: but among the righteous there is favour.*

In Genesis 12:1, God is speaking to Abraham and says,

> *Now the Lord had said unto Abram, Get thee out of thy country, and from thy kindred, and from thy father's house, unto a land that I will show thee: And I will make of thee a great nation, and I will bless thee, and make thy name great; and thou shalt be a blessing.*

The Amplified Bible says verse 2 this way:

> *And I will make you a great nation, and I will bless you [with an abundant increase of favors]...*

Notice the purpose of this covenant. God says that His intent for establishing covenant with Abraham was to give God an avenue by which He could bring blessings into Abram's life, and it would give God a channel to increase favor in the man's life. He said, *I will bless you with an abundant increase of favors.* In other words, God is saying, "I'd like to do favors for you, and I'd like to do them in abundance."

You may be thinking, "That's what He said to Abram, not me." Yes, but this also applied to the seed of Abram (or Abraham). In Galatians 3:29 it says, *And if ye be Christ's, then are ye Abraham's seed, and heirs according to the promise.* So you are entitled! Through this covenant, God has established a channel by which you are entitled to walk in the favor of God.

All you have to do is study Abraham's life and you see favor. Genesis 24:1 says,

And Abraham was old, and well stricken in age: and the Lord had blessed Abraham in all things.

God had favored him in all things. The favor of God in Abraham's life caused his wife's barren womb to conceive. The favor of God will even change medical reports. The favor of God will change what men say is impossible.

DECLARE FAVOR!

When God began ministering to me about His favor, I realized that I had let that revelation slip. The Lord said to me, "Son, you're not believing Me for favor like you used to. You could be walking in a whole lot more favor than what you're walking in if you'd believe Me for it. Consciously ask Me for favors." So I started.

I made up my mind, if I'm entitled to more favor, then I'm going to walk in it. I'm not just going to say, "Amen, hallelujah, praise God." No, I'm going to commit to it and actually walk in it. I do not let a day go by without confessing: "I walk in divine favor. The favor of God goes before me today, changing rules, regulations and policies."

I not only confess it for me but I confess it for my children. I confess that this family walks in the favor of God. And we do. Some of it is happening so instantly that it is overwhelming!

I challenge you to study favor and begin to confess the favor of God in your life. Be consistent with it. Don't just try it for three or four days and quit if you don't see any results. Be diligent about it. Revelation is going to come to you where the favor of God is concerned, and it is going to lift your self-esteem and your confidence. It's going to make you feel like you are somebody in the sight of God. Things that you've been struggling with for a long time are going to come to pass simply because you realize that you have favor with God.

You need to start declaring the favor of God. Confess the favor of God. Get up in the morning and say, "This is another day that the Lord has made, I will rejoice and be glad therein. The favor of God goes before me and surrounds me." You'll be amazed at doors that will start opening for you. Declare the favor of God! Decree the favor of God goes before you! And watch the doors open!

3

✤ ✤ ✤

Steps To Increasing God's Favor In Your Life

L uke 2:52 states, *And Jesus increased in wisdom and stature, and in favour with God and man.* From this verse, we see that we can increase in the favor of God. Let's see how this takes place in our lives.

1. CONSIDER YOUR WAYS

I entreated thy favour with my whole heart: be merciful unto me according to thy word. I thought on my ways, and turned my feet

unto thy testimonies.
                                    Psalm 119:58,59

The Psalmist is asking for more favor. Notice in verse 59, it reveals to us what he did to increase in favor. He said, *I thought on my ways...* Obviously, if you are going to ask for favor to be increased, then your lifestyle must be pleasing to God.

Your lifestyle has everything to do with favor increasing in your life. Remember what God said in Haggai 1:5-7,

> *Now therefore thus says the Lord of hosts; Consider your ways and set your mind on what has come to you. You have sown much, but you have reaped little; you eat, but you do not have enough; you drink, but you do not have your fill; you clothe yourselves, but no one is warm; and he who earns wages has earned them to put them in a*

bag with holes in it. Thus says the Lord of Hosts: Consider your ways...

(The Amplified Bible)

Consider your ways. Notice it didn't say, "Consider God's ways." There's nothing wrong with God's ways. The Amplified Version says, *...Consider your ways, (your previous and present conduct)...*(v.7) I did a study on this verse and found that **ways** could be defined as *course of action, methods and manners, conduct and behavior.* In other words, your course of action, your methods and manners, your conduct and your behavior have everything to do with whether or not you increase in the favor of God.

So if you want to increase in God's favor, then take an inventory of your ways. If you find things in your life that you know are not pleasing to God, then correct them. Take authority over them, and get them out of your life so that you can begin to walk in a greater level of God's favor.

2. CONTINUALLY SEEK GOD

Hear instruction, and be wise, and refuse it not. Blessed is the man that heareth me, watching daily at my gates, wailing at the posts of my doors. For whoso findeth me findeth life, and shall obtain favour of the Lord.

Proverbs 8:33-35

Findeth me... is a key to increasing in God's favor. Continually seek Him and keep your ears open to His voice and listen to His instructions for your life. Learn to be sensitive so you can hear His voice clearly. How do you find Him? By spending quality time with Him. Spend time reading His Word and praying in the Spirit so that you can get to know Him more intimately. The more intimate your fellowship with Him becomes, the more of His favor you'll experience.

3. __BE OBEDIENT__

Be obedient to God's instructions. Obviously, the more obedient you are to God, the more capability you have of increasing in His favor. People who are disobedient don't walk in favor. When you hear God's instructions, don't hesitate — be quick to obey. The person who will do that will not only find life, but he'll walk in a greater level of the favor of the Lord.

4. __HUNGER FOR TRUTH__

My son, forget not my law; but let thine heart keep my commandments: For length of days, and long life, and peace, shall they add to thee. Let not mercy and truth forsake thee: bind them about thy neck; write them upon the table of thine heart: So shalt thou find favour and good understanding in the sight of God and man.

Proverbs 3:1-4

WALKING IN DIVINE FAVOR

Create a hunger for truth. Seek it with all of your heart. When God sees how much you love truth, then favor will increase in your life. God delights in those who love truth. Remember, Jesus said that those who continue in His Word shall know the truth and the truth shall make them free.

5. <u>STRIVE FOR EXCELLENCE</u>

He that diligently seeketh good procureth favour: but he that seeketh mischief, it shall come unto him.

Proverbs 11:27

What does He mean by this? In other words, develop a lifestyle of seeking out that which is good and pleasing to God. Don't always look for the shortcuts in life. Look for the things that put a demand on your life to become the best you can possibly be. Look for ways to be a blessing to others. When you are favorable toward others then more favor comes to you.

6. DON'T EVER LOSE YOUR ZEAL FOR THE WORD

Whoso despiseth the word shall be destroyed: but he that feareth the commandment shall be rewarded. The law of the wise is a fountain of life, to depart from the snares of death. Good understanding giveth favour...

Proverbs 13:13-15

Notice he says, *Whoso despiseth the Word...* I've seen this happen to many Christians: "I'm so tired of studying the Word! I'm so tired of having to be in the Word all the time." The Word has become irksome to them. They've lost their zeal for the Word. They used to be zealous. They bought all the Christian books. They bought all the most inspirational tapes. They went to all the seminars. They couldn't get enough of the Word. But then, you don't see them quite as frequently. You notice they don't talk the Word like they used to.

Do you know anyone like this? They've lost their desire for the Word. According to this scripture, when you lose your zeal for the Word, you literally cut yourself off from increased favor. Never lose your zeal for the Word. Never lose your hunger for revelation knowledge and always desire understanding! Good understanding giveth favor. The more you understand God's ways, the more you're going to walk in His favor.

Favor In Your Time Of Trouble

Have you ever been overwhelmed by anything? Have you ever had a problem that consumed your mind 24 hours a day and there seemed to be no solution to it? In Psalm 102, we read about a man who is completely overwhelmed by his situation, he needs an answer from God, and he needs it immediately. See if you can relate.

> *Hear my prayer, O Lord, and let my cry come unto thee. Hide not thy face from me in the day when I*

am in trouble; incline thine ear unto me: in the day when I call answer me speedily (vv. 1,2).

He's getting right to the point. "God, I need an answer, and I need it real fast." He goes on to say in verses 3 to 13,

For my days are consumed like smoke, and my bones are burned as an hearth. My heart is smitten, and withered like grass; so that I forget to eat my bread. By reason of the voice of my groaning my bones cleave to my skin. I am like a pelican of the wilderness: I am like an owl of the desert. I watch, and am as a sparrow alone upon the house top.

Mine enemies reproach me all the day; and they that are mad against me are sworn against me. For I have eaten ashes like bread, and

mingled my drink with weeping, because of thine indignation and thy wrath: for thou hast lifted me up, and cast me down.

My days are like a shadow that declineth; and I am withered like grass. But thou, O Lord, shalt endure for ever; and thy remembrance unto all generations. Thou shalt arise, and have mercy upon Zion: **for the time to favour her, yea, the set time, is come.**

Notice that even though this man is overwhelmed by his adversity, he still recognizes that he is entitled to the favor of God. When many of us are faced with overwhelming situations, it's easy to become problem-minded rather than solution-minded. We tend to forget our covenant during a trial. Sometimes the problem can be so overwhelming that it's all you can think about. But notice in the midst of all of this, the Psalmist remembers that he is entitled to God's favor. The reason he knows he is entitled to it is because he's a covenant man.

Notice he says,

> *Thou shalt arise, and have mercy upon Zion: for the time to favour her, yea, the set time, is come.*

Once he begins to get his mind off the problem and starts thinking about the favor of God, he begins to speak more positively. He begins to talk about what God will do when He arises and what the favor of God will do when it comes on the scene. You need to realize that no matter what you are going through and no matter how severe it is, you are entitled to the favor of God, but you need to learn to expect that favor.

The Amplified says it this way,

> *...the moment designated has come...*

There is a moment designated for the favor of God to come.

Every time you have been under pressure, your situation looked impossible, and the Devil said, "There is no way," God always seemed to find a way. Isn't that right! Well, that was a manifestation of the favor of God. When you expect it to come, it will cause you to remain positive and change your perspective about your outcome.

TURNING YOUR TEST INTO A TESTIMONY

What once was an overwhelming test can be turned into a testimony. The Devil hopes you will forget that God's favor is available. He'd like for you to stay overwhelmed. Sometimes you just need to rehearse in your mind all the victories that you've had with God. Just think about them. This is a great weapon against the adversary, particularly when he is endeavoring to overwhelm you with a problem. Say to yourself, "Hey, wait a minute, I've been through adversity before. I've faced impossible situations before. Let me recall what God did the last time!"

When you start recalling how God delivered you, how God healed you and how God made a way, it causes your faith to be energized. Obviously, Satan doesn't want your faith to be energized because he knows your faith will overcome his attacks.

CHANGE YOUR ATTITUDE

Perspective is very important. When David was confronted with Goliath, he had a totally different perspective than his brothers. They saw a man too big to kill, but David saw a man too big to miss. Same giant, same problem, but a different perspective.

In the verses which we previously read, I believe the Psalmist starts out talking about how overwhelmed he is by his problems. But in a few moments, He begins to think about the mercy of God, the love of God, the favor of God and his position with God, and suddenly, his attitude changes.

He says, "The set time has come for Your favor to be manifested in my life." He expects it and God does it. God wants to pour out His favor. He wants to manifest His favor in your life, but it will not come until you have a change of attitude. Don't give in to the Devil, but expect the favor of God to show up in your life and it will every time.

EXPECT THE BEST

Quit saying, "Nothing good ever happens to me." You are highly honored and favored of God. That's the reason Paul calls you the elect of God. One definition of the word "elect" is "hand-picked." You are hand-picked by God. God accepted what Jesus did at Calvary; therefore, He accepted those for whom Jesus died and has made us righteous. You are in right standing with God; therefore, expect to walk in His favor.

I walk in humility, but at the same time, I expect to be favored. I expect doors to be opened for me that might not open for someone else. I expect to be blessed coming in and blessed going out. I expect to be blessed in the city and blessed in the field. Do you understand what I'm saying? Not because of what I've done but because of what Jesus has done.

You are an ambassador for Christ. Stop and think about it. Ambassadors of nations are highly favored and get preferential treatment. When they represent their nation, they get preferential treatment. They ride around in big cars with flags on the fenders, and they have escorts leading them to the embassy. Why? They are ambassadors.

We think of being an ambassador for Christ as some kind of second rate thing, but we represent the Kingdom of Almighty God. We're not talking about representing Nigeria or the United States or Canada. We're talking about representing a Kingdom that cannot be shaken, praise God. We're representing the Kingdom of the Most High God.

<u>RISE TO THE TOP</u>

The Bible reveals to us that when the favor of God is surrounding you like a shield then every adversity is turned into victory. We have an example in Genesis 39 of a man named Joseph who experienced adversity all around him. But, because the favor of God was on him and surrounded him, God turned every adversity into a victory.

Remember the story of how his brothers had deceived him and he was brought into captivity?

> *And the Lord was with Joseph, and he was a prosperous man; and he was in the house of his master the Egyptian. And his master saw that the Lord was with him, and that*

the Lord made all that he did to prosper in his hand.

Genesis 39:2,3

What a testimony! Even the Egyptians recognized that God's hand was upon him and that God made everything he did to prosper. "Why was the man prospering?" Because he was favored. Notice this happened even when he was in captivity. It didn't make any difference where Joseph was, he came out on top.

And Joseph found grace in his sight, and he served him: and he made him overseer over his house, and all that he had he put into his hand.

Genesis 39:4

The favor of God was on Joseph to the point that even his master, Potiphar, saw that this man was highly favored of God and he put him in charge of everything.

> *And it came to pass from the time that he had made him overseer in his house, and over all that he had, that the Lord blessed the Egyptian's house for Joseph's sake; and the blessing of the Lord was upon all that he had in the house, and in the field. And he left all that he had in Joseph's hand; and he knew not aught he had, save the bread which he did eat. And Joseph was a goodly person, and wellfavoured.*

Genesis 39:5,6

Here is a man who is supposed to be a slave and his master has turned everything over to him. He's so confident in Joseph's integrity and the favor of God that is on him that he just turns it all over to him and gives him total trust and confidence. Why? The favor of God was on Joseph.

Then, Potiphar's wife tries to seduce Joseph, and he won't have anything to do with her. Time and time again, she tries to seduce him, but his integrity will not allow him to compromise. Don't you wish there were more men and women like this today?

Because Joseph refuses her, she plots against him. When he constantly refuses her seduction, one day she grabs him as he's in her quarters and tries to seduce him. Still he will not yield. He will not compromise. He begins to run out, but she grabs his coat and hangs onto it. When his master returns, she lies about it and says that Joseph seduced her, showing him the coat for proof. Did you notice in this, Joseph never defended himself? He never said, "Your wife is lying." He didn't have to defend himself. He knew the favor of God was on him and that the favor of God would vindicate him. Of course the master believes his wife and Joseph ends up being thrown into prison, but that's not the end of the story.

> *But the Lord was with Joseph, and showed him mercy, and gave him favour in the sight of the keeper of the prison. And the keeper of the prison committed to Joseph's hand all the prisoners that were in the prison; and whatsoever they did there, he was the doer of it.*

> Genesis 39:21,22

He was thrown in prison, and then became the warden. That's favor! You cannot stop this man from being victorious. God's favor causes him to rise to the top every time. That's what the favor of God will do.

Verse 23 says:

> *The keeper of the prison looked not to any thing that was under his*

hand; because the Lord was with him, and that which he did, the Lord made it to prosper.

He just keeps being promoted! Notice what it says after Joseph interpreted Pharoah's dream.

And Pharaoh said unto Joseph, Forasmuch as God hath shown thee all this, there is none so discreet and wise as thou art:

And Pharaoh took off his ring from his hand, and put it upon Joseph's hand, and arrayed him in vestures of fine linen, and put a gold chain about his neck.

Genesis 41:39,42

This man was a slave, a prisoner, and a captive. His brothers deceived him, he was sold into slavery, and Pharoah winds up setting the entire land of Egypt under Joseph's oversight!

Verse 46 says:

And Joseph was thirty years old when he stood before Pharaoh king of Egypt...

This all happened to a young man because the favor of God was on him. That's what the favor of God will do. That's the reason you and I need to declare His favor. Even when the Devil tries to take us to the lowest pit, we will always rise to the top because of the favor of God.

GOD'S FAVOR ALWAYS PRODUCES VICTORIES

When you walk in favor, it will bring victories in your life that you cannot acquire in your own strength and in your own might.

Psalm 44:1-3 says,

> *We have heard with our ears, O God, our fathers have told us, what work thou didst in their days, in the times of old. How thou didst drive out the heathen with thy hand, and plantedst them; how thou didst afflict the people, and cast them out. For they got not the land in possession by their own sword, neither did their own arm save them: but thy right hand, and thine arm, and the light of thy countenance, because thou hadst a favour unto them.*

When they couldn't take the land by their own might, by their own strength, by their own intelligence or ability, God's favor came on them, and they were able to possess the land God had promised them.

You can either war in your own might, or you can rest in the favor of God. And when the favor of God goes before you, it will enable you to take possession of what is rightfully yours. The favor of God will help you win battles that you could never win in your own strength.

FAVOR PRODUCES CONFIDENCE

When the favor of God is upon you and goes before you, then you can walk with your head up high. You can walk with a sense of confidence and security knowing full well that God is on your side.

Psalm 89:17 says,

> *For thou art the glory of their strength: and in thy favour our horn shall be exalted.*

The Amplified says it this way,

For you are the glory of their strength [their proud adornment], and by Your favor our horn is exalted and we walk with up lifted faces!

The people of God shouldn't be walking around with their heads down in sorrow and defeat wondering, "My God, what are we ever going to do? How are we ever going to get out of this?" No, when God's favor is on you, you should be walking with an uplifted face. You should walk with a countenance of joy on you! Even though all of hell's power has broken loose in your life, you are confident that your God will deliver you. Amen.

When you walk in the favor of God, you don't bow down to Satan's pressure any more. He is no longer your master. It's time to stand up and tell him, "You're talking to someone who is highly favored of God. Are you trying to tell me this is impossible? Just watch. I love it when you say, 'impossible' because you don't know who you are talking to. I have favor with God. The favor of God surrounds me like a shield. It goes before me. It causes me to have a countenance of joy even in adversity. It enables me to laugh at you because I know your day is coming."

The Body of Christ needs to learn to walk in God's favor. We need to expect to increase in it, and have a positive attitude that every adversity will be turned into victory because the favor of God is upon us and we cannot be defeated.

5

⚜ ⚜ ⚜
⚜ ⚜

❖

FAVOR:
Above & Beyond

Recently, as I was studying the favor of God, I found that we have the right to walk in this favor above and beyond what I had even imagined. So far, you've seen a glimpse of what God's favor can produce in your life, but what you are about to read is going to broaden your thinking so much that you can't help but get excited.

Ephesians 2:7 says,

That in the ages to come he might show the exceeding riches of his grace in his kindness toward us through Christ Jesus.

He says that in the ages to come He wants to show (or demonstrate or manifest) the exceeding riches of His grace.

In other words, He wants to show us something that is tangible, something that you can see. The word "exceeding" in itself takes us out of the norm. "Exceeding" always expresses "above and beyond." This is going to be beyond any thing you've ever experienced before. To whom does He want to show this? Those who are in Christ Jesus. He's talking to you. God's going to show the exceeding riches of His grace to you.

The Amplified says it this way:

*He did this that He might clearly demonstrate through the ages to come the **immeasurable (limitless, surpassing)** riches of His free* *grace (His unmerited favor) in kindness and goodness of heart toward us in Christ Jesus.*

Notice three words: *immeasurable, limitless and surpassing.* Paul is saying, "I have experienced a level of God's grace, but in the ages to come, the grace that the last days church (us) will experience will surpass the grace that my generation is experiencing." (Author's Paraphrase).

The New International Version says it this way,

*In order that in the coming ages, He might show the **incomparable** riches of His grace, expressed in His kindness to us in Christ Jesus.*

So, we're going to experience His grace in ways that are **surpassing, incomparable, limitless,** and **immeasurable!** Obviously, this verse speaks of leaving the norm and moving into the realm of the "above and beyond."

The dictionary defines ***immeasurable*** as *boundless, vast, immense.* How far is vast? It is beyond anything we could possibly ask or think. ***Limitless*** is defined as *infinite.* The word ***surpassing*** is defined as *going beyond the limits, going beyond your range or your capacity.*

In the Old testament, when you see the words ***exceed, exceeding, or exceedingly***, it means *abundance, overflowing,* but it also means to *hang over.*

Exceeding also implies *not enough room to hold.* That explains why David said, "My cup runneth over!" He will pour out blessings that there will not be room enough to contain it all. You and I are about to experience the immeasurable, limitless, surpassing riches of His grace and His kindness.

Kindness always denotes favor. You could ask someone, "Would you do a favor for me?" And they reply, "Sure. What do you need?" That is an expression of kindness. It also expresses covenant relationship.

God is kind. He is full of compassion. He said that in the ages to come we will experience the immeasurable, surpassing, limitless expressions of His grace, His kindness and His favor.

The best way I know how to describe it is in comparison with my daughters and my grandchildren. I have two daughters, and while they were growing up, they experienced my grace. On the other hand, I have three grandsons and two granddaughters, but they experience my limitless, immeasurable, surpassing grace! In fact, my daughters ask me often, "Daddy, why do you let the grandkids do what you didn't let us do?" And I say, "You were under grace, but they are under surpassing grace!"

Now, I met all of their needs. I was kind to them. I proved my love to them. In fact, they wrote me notes all the time saying, "You're the best Daddy in the whole world." But my grandkids are over in that immeasurable, surpassing and limitless arena. They don't even have to ask for it. It's waiting for them when they come! Do you understand what I'm saying? That's what God is about to do with you and me! Hallelujah! He's going to show us favor like no other generation has ever experienced.

The Message translation says, "He's going to shower us with blessings." Do you know what that means? No more "mercy drops," as religious people often say, but showers of kindness and grace! *Grace* has been defined as *unmerited favor.* But another definition which I really like is *the ability of God coming on you enabling you to do what you can't do for yourself!* Isn't that good? *For by grace are ye saved.* I couldn't do that myself. It took grace. That's God's ability to do what I can't do in myself. So, let's tie that definition into Ephesians 2:7 (Amplified version),

> *He did this that He might clearly demonstrate through the ages to come the immeasurable (limitless, surpassing) riches of His free grace (His unmerited favor) in [His] kindness and goodness of heart toward us in Christ Jesus.*

This tells me that you and I will be able to accomplish things we have not been able to accomplish in the past. The ability of God will come on us to do what we've never been able to do before.

God is enabling the church to experience a set time of favor and grace. That doesn't mean we won't have opposition! No! We'll have opposition. We'll still have a Devil to deal with. But we're going to experience greater victories than we've ever experienced

The dictionary also defines the word *favor* as *to endorse, to support, to assist, to make easier, to provide with advantages, to show special privileges, or to be featured.*

Would you like a few of your faith projects to be a little easier? I didn't say you wouldn't have to use your faith. You're going to use your faith throughout eternity! But wouldn't it be wonderful if the sowing and reaping process was accelerated and things got easier?

In fact, the Spirit of God told me to write this down, and I encourage you to read it and keep it before you as encouragement: "Begin to expect Me to show up in everything you do and everywhere you go so I can support you, endorse you, assist you, make things easier, provide you with advantages, and grant special privileges."

I receive that! Now, you can read this book and say, "Wasn't that a nice little book

Brother Jerry wrote on favor," or you can receive this into your spirit, and lay hold of it until it becomes such a reality in your life that you begin walking in God's divine favor every day. Remember, you get exactly what you expect. Jesus said, "Be it done unto you according to your faith."

My faith is going to lay hold of this, praise God. I've already experienced the favor of God in my life but now I'm ready for the "surpassing, immeasurable, limitless" favor of God like never before.

FEATURE THIS

What does it mean "to be featured?" *To feature* implies *to give special prominence.* That's what favor will do. We see an example of this in Joshua 10. Remember Joshua and the children of Israel are engaged in warfare, and it says,

Then spake Joshua to the Lord in the day when the Lord delivered up the Amorites before the children of Israel, and he said in the sight of Israel, Sun, stand thou still upon Gibeon; and thou, Moon, in the valley of Ajalon.

And the sun stood still, and the moon stayed, until the people had avenged themselves upon their enemies. Is not this written in the book of Jasher? So the sun stood still in the midst of heaven and hasted not to go down about a whole day.

And there was no day like that before it or after it, that the Lord hearkened (featured, favored) *unto the voice of a man: for the Lord fought for Israel.*

Joshua 10:12-14

89

When God hearkened to Joshua's words, He favored him. There had never been a day like that before where God so "featured" one of His own. Can you imagine that? Talk about favor. When was the last time you told the sun to stand still because you needed more daylight? When was the last time you told the moon, "Be still. Don't move," and it obeyed you?

God allowed Joshua to experience His favor, His power, and His ability like no man had ever experienced before. You're going to have days where you'll hear yourself say, "I've never seen a day like this!" And this time you won't be referring to bad days, you'll be referring to good days!

God wants us to begin to expect Him to show up everywhere we go and in everything we do. Why? So He can endorse, support, assist, make easier, provide with advantages, grant special privileges, feature and give us special prominence.

Can you imagine how exciting your life will become when that starts happening? That's favor. God wants to make your life better. If there is any one thing believers need right now, it is deliverance from being stressed out. So many Christians are stressed out. They are on the verge of "burn out." Well, God wants to make your life easier. That doesn't mean a free ride. That doesn't mean you can just sit back and coast along, but it does mean that God will get involved in what you are doing and make life easier.

He wants to grant you special privileges and special advantages. He wants to feature you and give you special prominence. So, if you can imagine that kind of favor manifesting in your life, it is going to cause your life to become a tremendous adventure in faith.

The key to walking in this kind of favor is found in James 4:6 ...*God resisteth the proud, but giveth grace unto the humble.* The more you acknowledge that without Him you are nothing, the more of this kind of grace and favor you will experience.

Don't try to make these things happen yourself. All you'll do is tie God's hands. Just stay humble before God and allow that favor and grace to be given to you by reason of the pureness of your heart and humility.

I believe that God truly desires to demonstrate this kind of favor which He calls "immeasurable, limitless and surpassing" to a people who will no longer lean to the arm of the flesh but simply trust Him. It's time for God's favor to profusely abound, so let it happen and keep praising Him for it.

6

⚜ ⚜ ⚜
⚜ ⚜ ⚜

TEN BENEFITS
Of Walking In The Favor Of God

G od is saving the best for last. We are the ones who are going to experience the favor of God in its fullness. Get ready because there are going to be some changes around your house - favor is coming!

> *Thou shalt arise, and have mercy upon Zion: for the time to favour her, yea, the set time, is come.*

> Psalm 102:13

Notice the Psalmist said *the set time is come.* I believe that this is a key phrase. A "set time" would indicate that God's already programmed it in and no devil, or man, or government can change it. It is a set time. Notice what this "set time" is for: favor to come upon Zion. Zion is always symbolic of the church. In other words, there is a set time for favor to come upon the church like it has never experienced before.

Please understand that the Psalm is prophetic. Remember, we're reading the words of a prophet, not just a king, nor just a psalmist. He's seeing into the future.

Verse 15 says,

So the heathen shall fear the name of the Lord, and all the kings of the earth thy glory.

Now look at what Isaiah prophesied concerning the church in the future.

Arise, shine; for thy light is come, and the glory of the Lord is risen upon thee. For, behold, the dark-ness shall cover the earth, and gross darkness the people: but the Lord shall arise upon thee, and his glory shall be seen upon thee. And the Gentiles shall come to thy light, and kings to the brightness of thy rising.

Isaiah 60:1-3

He talks about the glory of God coming upon the church and it actually will be seen on us. When will this happen? When the world is in its darkest hour, the Church will be at its brightest.

Verse 16 pinpoints the time frame:

When the Lord shall build up Zion, [or the church] *he shall appear in his glory.*

Psalm 102:16

In other words, He's saying, "Before the appearing of the Lord, there will be a 'set time' of favor that the church will experience!" This "set time" will precede His appearing! And guess what? It's already happening! So, we're in it right now. The "ages to come" that Paul spoke about in Ephesians 2:7 have come. Therefore, we should expect the favor of God on us like never before.

FAVOR PRODUCES WEALTH

Lift up thine eyes round about, and see: all they gather themselves together, they come to thee: thy sons shall come from far, and thy daughters shall be nursed at thy side. Then thou shall see, and flow together, and thine heart shall fear, and be enlarged; because the abundance of the sea shall be converted unto thee, the forces of the Gentiles shall come unto thee.

Isaiah 60:4,5

In the Hebrew, the word *forces* is translated *wealth*. Wealth is associated or connected to favor. If you study your Bible, you'll see that many who walked in the favor of God experienced financial blessings as well. Favor produces wealth.

We know that God has prophesied that a financial inversion will take place in the earth before the appearing of the Lord Jesus, and that the wealth of the sinner has been laid up for the just. So, if this "set time" of favor has come, then the church can anticipate greater wealth and finances. It will be experienced by those who are faithful and living righteously according to the Word of God. If you are one of those, then you are a candidate for greater finances than you've ever experienced before in your life. Of course, this only applies to tithers. If you aren't a tither, then He's certainly not going to cause this financial inversion to come on you. But on the other hand, if you are a tither, then get ready because He's going to pile it on those He can trust!

I want you to see a pattern for this in 2 Chronicles 1:12 when Solomon was given the assignment to build the temple.

> *Wisdom and knowledge is granted unto thee; and I will give thee riches, and wealth, and honour,* (or favor) *such as none of the kings have had that have been before thee, neither shall there any after thee have the like.*

God is saying, "I'm about to put favor on you like no one before you has ever walked in."

> *And the king made silver and gold at Jerusalem as plenteous as stones...*
> 2 Chronicles 1:15

Can you imagine having as much gold and silver as you have gravel in your driveway?

Send me therefore a man cunning to work in gold... Send me also cedar trees, fir trees...

2 Chronicles 2:7,8

In other words, during a time of favor, God supplies everything you need to get the job done.

*Even to prepare me **timber in abundance:** for the house which I am about to build shall be wonderful great.*

2 Chronicles 2:9

Do you need timber in abundance? I do! We're building, building, building and we need timber in abundance. Are you believing for a house? Then, you need timber in abundance. Well, favor produces it!

And we will cut wood out of Lebanon, **as much as thou shalt need...**

2 Chronicles 2:16

We're not going to "barely get by" any more. We're not going to have to cut any corners. No, when favor comes, you'll have "as much as thou shalt need."

Thus all the work that Solomon made for the house of the Lord was finished...

2 Chronicles 5:1

And the next thing that will happen is the appearing of the Lord in His glory:

It came even to pass, as the trumpeters and singers were as one, to make one sound to be heard in praising and thanking the Lord; and when they lifted up their voice with the trumpets and cymbals and instruments of music, and praised the Lord, saying, For he is good; for his mercy endureth for ever: that then the house was filled with a cloud, even the house of the Lord;

So that the priests could not stand to minister by reason of the cloud: for the glory of the Lord had filled the house of God.

2 Chronicles 5:13,14

...the time to favour her, yea, the set time, is come.

...When the Lord shall build up Zion, he shall appear in his glory.

Psalm 102:13,16

Notice what precedes the appearing of the Lord: a "set time of favor." We just read about a pattern for that when Solomon built the temple. Notice God granted him honor and favor and with it came riches, wealth and honor. Not only that, but with it came the right people, all that he needed, abundance, plenty, expertise, quality, talent, and anointing. I submit to you that we are in that set time and that's what we can expect.

Can you imagine how exciting this is going to be as we lay hold of it and begin to walk in it? God is saving the best for last. Now, I want to give you 10 major benefits that I've discovered from the Word of God to those who walk in God's divine favor. These are benefits you can expect when the favor of God is on your life.

Study each of these carefully and begin to confess them everyday. God confirms His Word when we are bold to declare it.

10 BENEFITS OF
THE FAVOR OF GOD

1. Favor produces supernatural increase and promotion.

But the Lord was with Joseph, and showed him mercy, and gave him favour in the sight of the keeper of the prison.

Genesis 39:21

2. Favor produces restoration of everything that the enemy has stolen from you.

And I will give this people favour in the sight of the Egyptians: and it shall come to pass, that, when ye go, ye shall not go empty.

Exodus 3:21

3. Favor produces honor in the midst of your adversaries.

And the Lord gave the people favour in the sight of the Egyptians. Moreover the man Moses was very great in the land of Egypt, in the sight Pharaoh's servants, and in the sight of the people.

Exodus 11:3

4. Favor produces increased assets, especially in the area of real estate.

And of Naphtali he said, O Naphtali, satisfied with favour, and full with the blessing of the Lord, possess thou the west and the south.

Deuteronomy 33:23

5. Favor produces great victories in the midst of great impossibilities.

For it was of the Lord to harden their hearts, that they should come against Israel in battle, that he might destroy them utterly, and that they might have no favour, but that he might destroy them, as the Lord commanded Moses.

Joshua 11:20

6. Favor produces recognition, even when you seem the least likely to receive it.

And Saul sent to Jesse, saying, Let David, I pray thee, stand before me; for he hath found favour in my sight.

I Samuel 16:22

7. Favor produces prominence
and preferential treatment.

*And the king loved Esther above
all the women, and she obtained
grace and favour in his sight more
than all the virgins; so that he set
the royal crown upon her head,
and made her queen instead of
Vashti.*

Esther 2:17

8. Favor produces petitions granted
even by ungodly civil authorities.

*If I have found favour in the sight
of the king, and if it please the king
to grant my petition, and to per-
form my request, let the king and
Haman come to the banquet that I
shall prepare for them, and I will
do tomorrow as the king hath said.*

Esther 5:8

9. Favor causes policies, rules, regulations and laws to be changed and reversed to your advantage.

And said, If it please the king, and if I have found favour in his sight, and the thing seem right before the king, and I be pleasing in his eyes, let it be written to reverse the letters devised by Haman the son, of Hammedatha the Agagite, which he wrote to destroy the Jews which are in all the king's provinces.

Esther 8:5

10. Favor produces battles won which you won't even fight because God will fight them for you.

For they got not the land in possession by their own sword, neither did their own arm save them:

*but thy right hand, and thine arm,
and the light of thy countenance,
because thou hadst a favour unto
them.*

Psalm 44:3

So, these are 10 major benefits that I've seen in my study of the Favor of God! The Psalmist says that we are compassed about by the favor of God. One translation says, "It surrounds us." When you get up every morning, anticipate the favor of God going before you. Anticipate the favor of God surrounding you. Expect favor to open doors every day. Expect these benefits to manifest in your life.

Remember you will get exactly what you expect. If you expect God's favor to surround you, then you will see it. If you don't, then it won't. Your expectations are more powerful than any negative thing that Satan can put before you. They will override the negative no matter how often they may manifest in your life. So expect God's favor in your life and watch what it will do. The set time has come so tap into it!

7

FAVOR
And The Desires
Of Your Heart

*Delight thyself also in the Lord;
and he shall give thee the desires
of thine heart.*

Psalms 37:4

I've found out that favor will work, not only in spiritual things, but it will work in producing the desires of your heart. I discovered that the desires of your heart are very dear to the heart of the Father, particularly, if your lifestyle is pleasing to Him. When your lifestyle is pleasing to Him, then your desires will line up with His will. Your desires aren't going to be sinful or something that is out of character in order for a lifestyle to be pleasing to God.

I found this out in my own life regarding the things that I enjoy. My background was in the automotive business. I owned and operated my own automotive paint and body shop. I went into business for myself as a young man and enjoyed working on and restoring old cars.

My dad was an automotive paint and body man. He taught me the trade when I was a young boy. After Carolyn and I married, I went to school at night trying to continue my college education and worked at a number of dealerships. But my ambition was to have my own business.

My Dad and I loved racing. Dad built hot rods when I was growing up. He raced and he built several hot rods that were featured in

"Hot Rod" magazine back in the fiftics. My Dad loved speed, and since I was a kid who loved fast cars, I had it made. We always had hot rods and race cars.

Dad was always customizing, hot-rodding, and making cars faster. When you are a kid who loves that kind of thing, your Dad becomes your best friend. I would rather have been with my Dad than any of my classmates because he loved everything I loved. And everything I loved had to be fast. I started out with bicycles, but they had to be the fastest. My motor scooter had to be the fastest. My motorcycle had to be the fastest. My whole life was centered around automobiles and racing.

I grew up with the ambition of having my own business and spending the rest of my life on a race track somewhere. When I was growing up, the ultimate race was the Indy 500. I wanted to go so bad, I could hardly stand it. My High School graduation present was going to be a trip to the Indy 500.

Well, Dad tried to get tickets and did everything he knew to do, but we were not able to go. He and I both were very disappointed. I appreciated the fact that he did all that he could, and I understood, but I still wanted to go. It was a desire of my heart and it never left me.

Well, a few years ago, I was asked by a friend of mine who works for the Sheriff's Department in Marion County, Indiana to come and do a meeting in Indianapolis, in the inner city. So, I went and we had a great meeting. Afterwards, he said, "I want you to come to the Sheriff's Department. There is something I want to do for you." I said, "Fine."

So, he picked me up and took me to the Sheriff's Department. When I got there they asked me to go into this room and stand in a certain spot on the floor and they took my picture. In a few minutes, they handed me an ID that had my picture on it and a badge and they said, "Brother Jerry, we want you to know how much we appreciate you coming here and helping us in the inner city. We just want you to know that as a token of our appreciation, you are now an Honorary Deputy Sheriff in Marion County, Indiana." I received an official badge.

My friend said, "Brother Jerry, is there anything in Indianapolis that you would like to do?"

I said, "Yes sir. There is something that I have wanted to do for a long time - go to the Indy 500!"

When the favor of God is on your life, God does exceeding abundantly above all that you can ask or think. I want you to know that hc picked me up in a squad car and took me to the Indy. There were nearly half a million people that showed up for the race. Most people have to fight the crowd all morning just trying to get in. Not me! I sat in the sheriff's car thinking to myself, *Favor, favor, preferential treatment, glory to God!*

He took me right up to the gate where the garages, cars, mechanics and drivers are. There were thousands of people standing around this gate just pressed against each other trying to see a car inside one of those garages. They were hoping one of the drivers would walk out.

I showed them my badge and I went right through that gate. I went right into the garages, and I got to watch them tune the cars before the race. I've got pictures of me putting fuel in Mario Andretti's car. I've got pictures of me shaking hands with A.J. Foyt. This is a dream come true and it's all because of the favor of God.

One year, I even got to take my Dad. His dream came true too. There we were doing what we had dreamed of doing way back in 1964. God is so good. He never ceases to amaze me. He cares about what you care about. All He asks is that we delight ourselves in Him and He will give us the desires of our heart.

Now, I realize that going to the Indy may not be your heart's desire, but my point is this: God loves you so much that whatever your heart's desire might be, He will grant it if you'll just live for Him and serve Him faithfully. You have favor with God. Don't ever forget it and don't let anyone talk you out of it.

I pray that this book has encouraged you and stirred your spirit to believe for the manifestation of God's favor in your life everyday. If you will, then you are headed for the greatest adventures in faith that you've ever experienced.

I encourage you to make this confession right now:

In the name of Jesus, by the authority of God's Word, from this moment forward, I do not look at myself in the natural, but according to the Word of God. I see myself the way God sees me. I am highly favored of the Lord. I am crowned with glory and honor. I take authority over condemnation, over guilt, over shame, over inferiority. That's not of God. I break it's power over me.

In Jesus name, I declare by faith, I walk in favor. I have preferential treatment. I refuse to allow condemnation in my life. From this moment forward, my self-esteem and my self-image shall rise and be in accordance with God's Word. I'll not be high minded. I'll walk in humility. But I know who I am in Christ and I fully expect the treatment that is afforded to those who are highly favored.

In Jesus' name, every morning when I arise, I will declare, 'This is the day that the Lord has made, I will rejoice and be glad in it and I'll walk in favor!' Doors will open for me that men say are impossible to open. Today, this very day, I expect the favor of God to go before me.

In Jesus' Name, I am honored by my Father. I am special to Him. I am the object of His affection. And if God loves me, nothing can separate me from His love. I am favored of the Lord, in Jesus' Name. Amen.

About The Author

Dr. Jerry Savelle is a noted author, evangelist, pastor and teacher who travels extensively throughout the United States, Canada, and around the globe. He is president of Jerry Savelle Ministries International, a ministry of many outreaches devoted to meeting the needs of Believers all over the world.

Well-known for his balanced Biblical teaching, Dr. Savelle has conducted seminars, crusades and conventions for over thirty years as well as ministering in thousands of churches and fellowships. He is in great demand today because of his inspiring message of victory and faith and his vivid, and often humorous, illustrations from the Bible. He teaches the uncompromising Word of God with a power and an authority that is exciting, but with a love that delivers the message directly to the spirit man.

In addition to his international headquarters in Crowley, Texas, Dr. Savelle is also founder of JSMI-United Kingdom, JSMI-South Africa, JSMI-Asia, JSMI-Tanzania, JSMI-Australia and JSMI-Botswana. In 1994, he established the Heritage of Faith Bible Institute and School of World Evangelism. It is a two-year school for the preparation of ministers to take the Gospel of Jesus Christ to the nations of the world. He also has a Bible School in Wales (United-Kingdom) and more recently pastors a church with his wife, Carolyn, in Crowley, Texas, called Heritage of Faith Christian Center.

The missions outreaches of his ministry extend to over 50 countries around the world.

Dr. Savelle has written many books and has an extensive video and cassette teaching tape ministry and a nation-wide television broadcast. Thousands of books, tapes, and videos are distributed around the world every year through Jerry Savelle Ministries International.

FOR THOSE WHO DON'T KNOW JESUS, WOULD YOU LIKE TO KNOW HIM?

If you were to die today, where would you spend eternity? If you have accepted Jesus Christ as your personal Lord and Savior, you can be assured that when you die, you will go directly into the presence of God in Heaven. If you have not accepted Jesus as your personal Lord and Savior, is there any reason why you can't make Jesus the Lord of your life right now? Please pray this prayer out loud, and as you do, pray with a sincere and trusting heart, and you will be born again.

Dear God in Heaven,

I come to you in the Name of Jesus to receive salvation and eternal life. I believe that Jesus is Your Son. I believe that He died on the cross for my sins, and that you raised Him from the dead. I receive Jesus now into my heart and make Him the Lord of my life. Jesus, come into my heart. I welcome you as my Lord and Savior. Father, I believe Your Word that says I am now saved. I confess with my mouth that I am saved and born again. I am now a child of God.

To order related material,
call, write or visit our website
for further information.

Jerry Savelle Ministries International
P.O. Box 748
Crowley, TX 76036
817/297-3155
www.jsmi.org

Other Books By Jerry Savelle

HERITAGE
OF FAITH

BIBLE INSTITUTE

& SCHOOL OF

WORLD EVANGELISM

Dear Friend,

Carolyn and I count it an honor to be involved in raising up students who will preach the uncompromised Word of God to the nations of the world. Heritage of Faith Bible Institute and School of World Evangelism is the fulfillment of a dream that was birthed in my spirit many years ago, and I am extremely excited about the potential we now have to train up students in an atmosphere charged with faith!

Our desire is to see each student develop a passion for God and a passion for souls. We endeavor to impart into each student the spirit of revival and help them become equipped and ready to participate in the last days move of God, bringing multitudes into His Kingdom.

If you are looking for a unique opportunity to increase your knowledge of the scriptures and find your place in God's plan, then I trust you will prayerfully consider our school.

Sincerely,

Dr. Jerry Savelle

A P P L I C A T I O N
R E Q U E S T   F O R M

Please send me an application for
Heritage of Faith Bible Institute and
School of World Evangelism

Name _____

Address _____

City/State _____

Zip/Telephone _____

To receive your FREE application packet, please
complete this form, tear it out and mail today.

Heritage of Faith
Bible Institute and School
of World Evangelism
P.O. Box 999
Crowley, TX 76036
817/297-2243 M-F 8:30-5:00 (CST)

NOTES

NOTES